TREE

1. Basecoat ornament using Snow White. Paint back and sides using a mix of Indian Turquoise + Snow White (1:2).
2. Transfer drawing to surface and follow diagram to paint areas.
3. Sideload flat brush with extender and Leaf Green and shade around edges of tree and around orange and red ornaments. Repeat sideload with Indian Turquoise and shade around outside edge of ornament. See photo on page 5.
4. Paint swirls using a mix of Yellow Green + Leaf Green + White (2:1:1). Repaint over the top of swirl using Yellow Green + White (1:1) to add highlights.
5. Snowflakes are Snow White.
6. Add highlight on edges of tree using Tangerine. See photo for placement.
7. Use liner brush and Lamp Black or Black permanent marker to add ornament hanger.
8. Add highlights to dots on ornaments as follows: Petal Pink on Fuchsia dots, a mix of Tangerine + Snow White (1:1) on Tangerine dots and a mix of Leaf Green + Yellow Green + Lemonade (1:6:1) on Green dots.
9. Add a pattern of snowflakes on back of ornament, if desired.

Colors

1. White
2. Black
3. Leaf Green
4. Pumpkin
5. Tangerine
6. Moon Yellow
7. Marigold
8. Petal Pink
9. Indian Turquoise
10. Indian Turquoise/White 1:2
11. Cadmium Red/Royal Fuchsia/Pumpkin 1:1:1
12. Cadmium Red/White 1:1
13. Cadmium Red/White 1:2
14. Tangerine/White 1:1
15. Yellow Green/White 1:1
16. Yellow Green/Leaf Green/White 2:1:1
17. Leaf Green/Yellow Green/Lemonade 1:6:1
18. Royal Fuchsia/Petal Pink 1:1
19. Petal Pink/White 1:1
20. Royal Fuchsia

Paint swirls #16, repaint, highlight with #15.
Paint snowflakes #1 White.

Colors

1. White
2. Black
3. Bright Green
4. Marigold
5. Moon Yellow
6. Pumpkin
7. Tangerine
8. Honey Brown
9. Indian Turquoise/White 1:6
10. Indian Turquoise/White 1:2
11. Bright Green/White 1:2
12. Bright Green/White 1:3
13. Royal Fuchsia/Petal Pink 1:1
14. Cadmium Red/Royal Fuchsia/Pumpkin 1:1:1
15. Indian Turquoise

Paint eyes, nose, and mouth #2 Black.
Paint swirls #1 White.
Shade edges of ornament and around snowman using Indian Turquoise and *Brush 'n Blend*.

Colors

1. White
2. Black
3. Petal Pink
4. Bright Green
5. Tangerine
6. Royal Fuchsia/Petal Pink 5:1
7. Pumpkin
8. Yellow Green/Bright Green 3:1
9. Yellow Green/White 1:1
10. Petal Pink/White 1:2
11. Indian Turquoise/White 1:2
12. Indian Turquoise/White 1:6
13. Moon Yellow
14. Royal Fuchsia/Petal Pink 1:3
15. Tangerine/White 1:1

Paint swirls #12 with #1 highlights.

Colors

1. White
2. Black
3. Honey Brown
4. Medium Flesh
5. Tangerine
6. Pumpkin
7. Yellow Green
8. Indian Turquoise/White 1:1
9. Indian Turquoise/White 1:6
10. Primary Yellow
11. Tangerine/Primary Yellow/White 1:1:1
12. Primary Yellow/White 1:1
13. Cadmium Red/Royal Fuschia/Pumpkin 1:1:1
14. Royal Fuchsia
15. Royal Fuchsia/Petal Pink 1:3
16. Petal Pink/White 1:1
17. Petal Pink
18. Yellow Green/White 1:1

Paint eyes and dots on muzzle #2 Black.

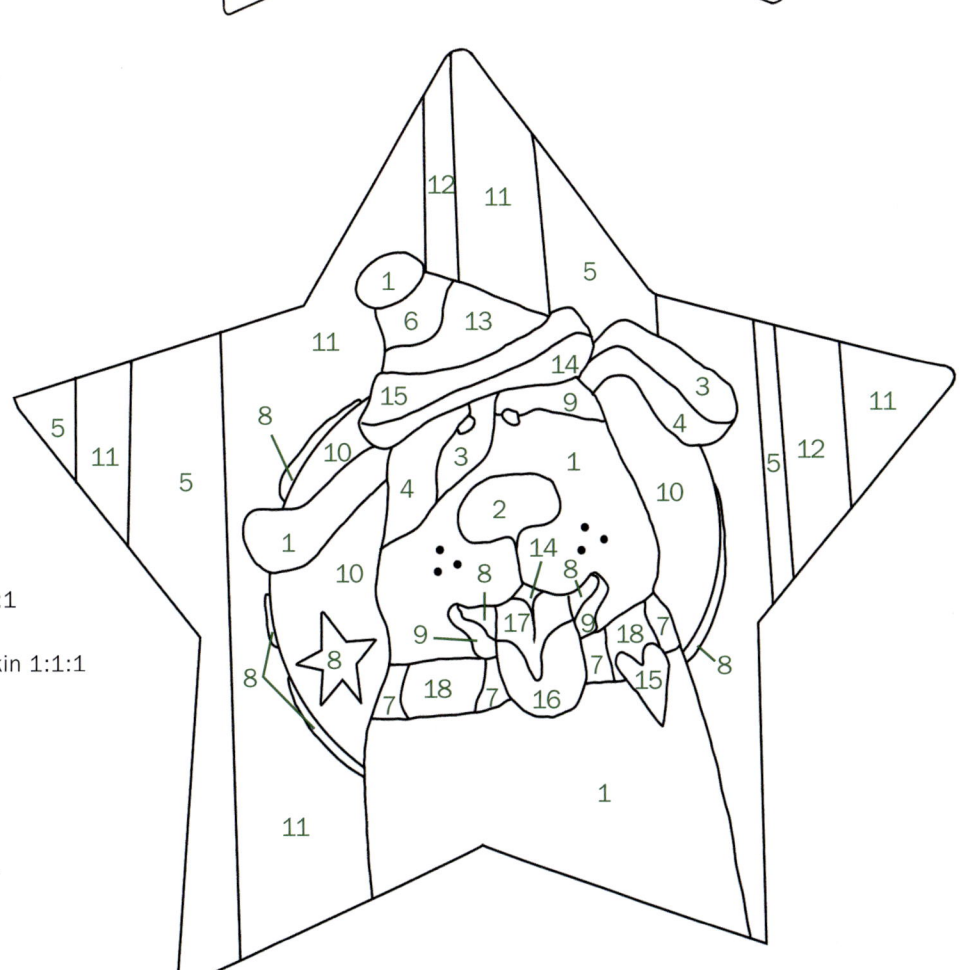

The Joy of the Season

These penguins are enjoying the simple pleasures of the holiday season: a hug from a friend, singing a favorite carol, and traveling to a friend's house loaded down with gifts. May you also enjoy these gifts with friends and family.

Jane Allen

Materials

SURFACE
Puffed tin ornaments: Mitten – FT-2104, Stocking – FT-2094, Tree – FT-2134 available from Della and Company (see resources, page 56)

PALETTE
DecoArt Americana Acrylics: Blue Chiffon, Burnt Umber, Deep Teal, French Vanilla, Lamp Black, Neutral Grey, Raw Sienna, Salem Blue, Sapphire, Soft Black, Soft Lilac, Spa Blue, Tangerine, Warm White
DecoArt Craft Twinkles: Crystal

BRUSHES
Loew-Cornell, La Corneille Golden Taklon: #2 round (Series 7000), 10/0 liner (Series 7350), ½" angular shader (Series 7400), ¾" wash/glaze (Series 7550)

ADDITIONAL SUPPLIES
DecoArt Multipurpose Sealer, DecoArt Americana Acrylic Sealer/Finisher, Matte

Preparation

1. Prepare following general instruction for tin on page 2.
2. On your first basecoat, mix your paint with multipurpose sealer (1:1). Basecoat front and back of stocking and mitten Chiffon Blue and tree Spa Blue.
3. Transfer patterns on page 10 using grey transfer paper.

Painting

TREE ORNAMENT
1. Shade top of tree and under each tier and base with Salem Blue. Using tip of round brush and Chiffon Blue, tap snow on branches, top of tree, and over feet and ground; reinforce with Warm White.
2. Basecoat belly and markings with Warm White and the rest of penguins with Soft Black. Shade dark areas with Lamp Black; highlight with Neutral Grey. Paint eye with Neutral Grey, place marking of Tangerine in eye with tip of liner brush, and highlight with Warm White. Paint markings with Tangerine; float under chin with Tangerine.

MITTEN AND STOCKING ORNAMENTS
1. Float Salem Blue a third of the way down the ornaments from the top. Reinforce with Sapphire Blue. Float across horizon with Soft Lilac. Using Warm White and a slip-slap motion, paint some clouds in the sky.
2. Basecoat belly and markings with Warm White and the rest of penguins with Soft Black. Highlight with Neutral Grey. Paint eye with Neutral Grey, place marking of Tangerine in eye with tip of liner brush, and highlight with Warm White. Paint markings with Tangerine, float under chin with Tangerine.
3. Basecoat sheet music with French Vanilla and shade with Raw Sienna. Basecoat basket with Raw Sienna and shade with Burnt Umber. Paint cloth French Vanilla; using tip of liner brush, paint small dots around edge. Paint fish Tangerine and eye Soft Black.
4. Using liner brush and Deep Teal, paint tree trunk then pull small stroke from top down to form branches; float over tree to strengthen color. Paint over bottom of trunk with Burnt Umber.
5. Paint star and snow with Warm White. Shade snow with Salem Blue. Using round brush and Warm White, paint randomly over snow allowing shadow to show through in places.

Finishing

1. Flyspeck ornaments with Warm White.
2. Paint over snow, star, and trees with Crystal twinkles. Varnish with matte sealer/finisher.
3. Use ribbon or rattail satin cording for hanger.

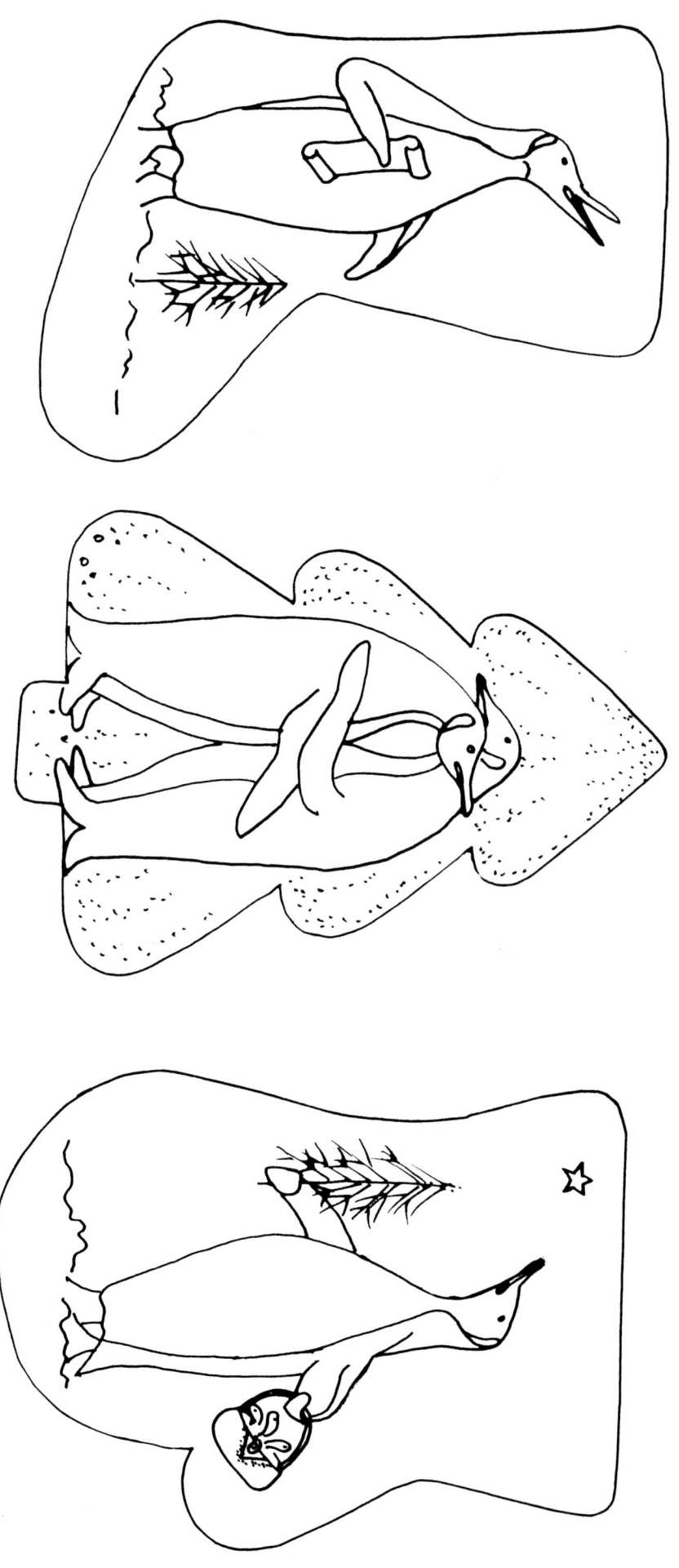

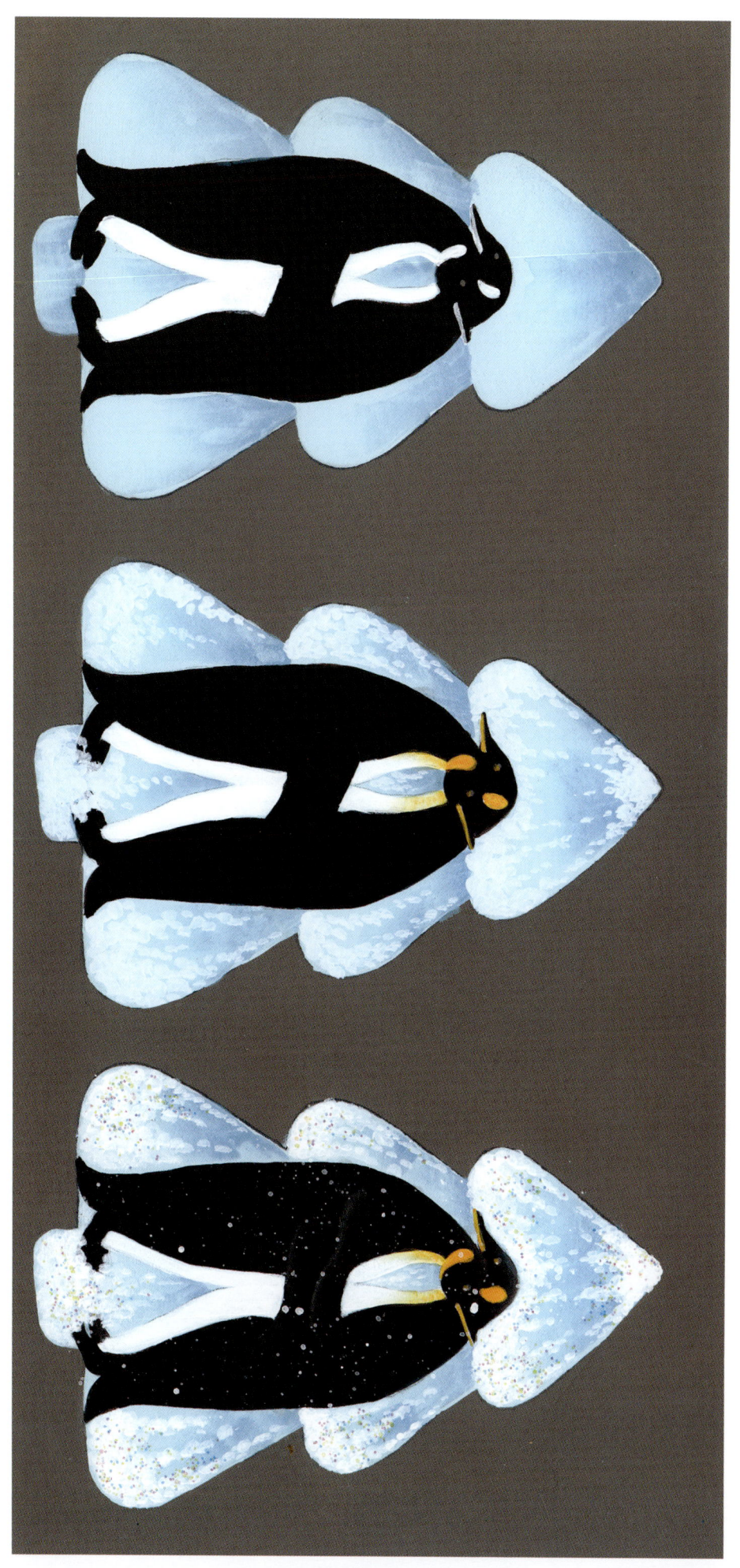

Kitty Kapers

There are sparkly balls, colorful ribbons and sweet treats. What's not to like about Christmas—especially for a mischievous cat! Paint these ornaments for your tree or for a special gift tag for your favorite cat-lover.

Sharon Chinn, CDA

Materials

SURFACE
Three mini wooden ironing board blanks, No. Wood-MIBO (2½" x 8⅛"), available from Sweet Patoodies (see resources, page 56)

PALETTE
DecoArt Americana Acrylics: Avocado, Avocado Dip, Burnt Umber, Cherry Red, Cool White, Deep Burgundy, Lamp Black, Neutral Grey, Sand
DecoArt Hot Shots – Fiery Red

BRUSHES
Royal & Langnickel: ¼" and ½" angular (Fusion Series 3160); #2 shader (Fusion Series 2150), 20/0 liner (Fusion Series 3595); #6, #8 short rounds (Royal Sable Series 5005)

ADDITIONAL SUPPLIES
00 permanent black pen; *DecoArt Americana Acrylic Sealer/Finisher Spray,* Matte; *DecoArt Americana Dura-Clear Varnish,* Matte; thin jute twine

Preparation

Note: Refer to all manufacturers' labels for proper product usage.
1. Sand ornaments and wipe with a soft cloth.
2. Base back of ornaments and edges with Burnt Umber. Base front with Sand. When dry, sand lightly to smooth grain.
3. Transfer main pattern lines (see page 17); transfer details as needed.

Painting

Note: For the purposes of this project, the shading generally falls to the left and bottom edges or along an edge that is "behind" the object in front. Highlighting generally falls to the right and top edges or along an edge that is "in front" of the object behind.

HAVE A BALL ON CHRISTMAS!
Ornament
1. Using wet-on-wet basecoat technique, base ornament with Fiery Red in highlight area toward top right, blend into Cherry Red for medium value, and Deep Burgundy for shadowed area at bottom. This may take 2-3 coats to get good coverage; just let it dry completely between coats so layers don't lift.
2. Topper on ornament is Neutral Grey + Sand (a light grey). Float shading along sides with Neutral Grey. Float highlight along inner flutes with Sand. Outline with Cool White. Float shading along bottom edge of ornament with Black Plum.
3. Strengthen highlight on ornament by drybrushing with Fiery Red + Cool White (about 1" in diameter). Then add a little more Cool White and drybrush a stronger highlight within this area (about ½" in diameter).
4. Float a reflected highlight at bottom of ornament with Neutral Grey + Sand. Re-float with a transparent wash of Avocado Dip. Also float upper right edge of ornament with Avocado Dip to accent.
5. Line and dot snowflake highlight with Cool White.
6. Line hook and loop with Neutral Grey. Line left and bottom edges of topper with Lamp Black, then highlight by lining with Cool White.

7. Finish ornament by sketchily outlining with a 00 permanent black pen.

Cat
1. Basecoat cat with Neutral Grey, jagging edges a little to create a furry look. Nose is Cherry Red + a little Sand. Float shade left side of nose with Deep Burgundy. Float highlight top of nose with a little Fiery Red + Sand. Dot upper right with Cool White to highlight.
2. Float Lamp Black shading on cat. Float Sand highlighting.
3. Float some pink (Cherry Red + Sand) inside ears.
4. Paint eyes with Cool White, iris with Avocado, and pupil with Lamp Black. Shade across the top of the eye with a narrow float of Lamp Black. Add two dots of Cool White in upper right and fine crescent in lower left of each eye to highlight.
5. Drybrush stronger highlights on cat with Sand + Neutral Grey between eyes and on forehead, middle of tail, and on feet/paws.
6. Fur strokes are made using a 20/0 liner and paint that is thinned with water to an inky consistency. First line with Neutral Grey pulling fur out over edges of cat. Then lighten fur strokes with Neutral Grey + Sand for highlight areas. Finally pull some Cool White strokes up the nose and out over forehead for strongest highlights.
7. Accent cat by floating a little Avocado Dip on left side of face and top of right ear, top of left front paw, and top of middle toe on right front paw, and left rear foot. Float a little Deep Burgundy on bottom edge of tail and in shadow of right rear paw.
8. Dot cheeks with Cool White to highlight.
9. Finish cat by sketchily outlining with a 00 permanent black pen.

Pine Branch
1. Line branch with Avocado + Deep Burgundy.
2. Using liner brush pull needles with Avocado. Repeat with Avocado Dip. Work around cat's ear and pull some of the needles over the ear a little.
3. Finish by pulling some needles using a 00 permanent black pen to add a little definition.
4. Dot berries with Cherry Red. When dry, highlight with a smaller dot of *Hot Shots* – Fiery Red.

Background
1. Drybrush some Avocado and Deep Burgundy around left and lower edges to frame the design.

CANDY CANE FOR SANTA
Candy Cane
1. Basecoat with Cool White. Float shade sides with Neutral Grey.
2. Paint stripes with Fiery Red (two coats). Float shade sides with Cherry Red, then finally with Deep Burgundy.
3. Green pinstripes are Avocado; float shade the edges here and there with Avocado.
4. Drybrush center of cane with Cool White for final highlight.
5. Finish by sketchily outlining with a 00 permanent black pen.
6. For the tag Float edges with Cool White.
7. Outline edges, lettering, and string bow around cane with 00 permanent black pen.

Cat
1. Basecoat cat with Neutral Grey, except muzzle, chin, and feet; basecoat them Cool White.
2. Nose is Fiery Red. Float shade left side of nose with Cherry Red. Dot upper right with Cool White to highlight.
3. Float Lamp Black shading on cat's grey parts. Float Neutral Grey shading on cat's muzzle and feet. Darken shading where mouth meets muzzle with a little Lamp Black.
4. Float Cool White highlighting on cat's front paws, ears, and top of tail. It will take a few coats on front paws to get good coverage; just let dry between coats.
5. Paint eyes with Cool White, iris with Avocado Dip and pupil with Lamp Black. Shade across the top of the eye with a narrow float of Lamp Black. Add two dots of Cool White in upper right and a fine crescent in lower left of each eye to highlight.
6. Drybrush highlight in center of forehead with Cool White and a little on the right leg.
7. Basecoat bow with Fiery Red. Float shade with Cherry Red, then deepen shading with Deep Burgundy.
8. Finish cat by sketchily outlining and adding detail with a 00 permanent black pen.

Background
1. Drybrush some Avocado and Deep Burgundy around left and lower edges to frame the design.

Pine Branch
1. Line branch with Avocado + Deep Burgundy.
2. Using a liner brush pull needles with Avocado. Repeat with Avocado Dip. Finish by pulling some needles using a 00 permanent black marker pen to add a little definition.
3. Dot berries with Cherry Red. When dry, highlight with a smaller dot of Fiery Red.

GUARDING THE PRESENTS
Presents
1. Basecoat bottom present with Avocado Dip; add red stripes with Deep Burgundy. Then drybrush over with Fiery Red to highlight. Green pinstripes are Avocado. Float left and bottom edges with Avocado. Float top edge with Sand to highlight.
2. Basecoat middle present with Fiery Red. Float left and bottom edges with Cherry Red to shade. Drybrush a little Sand toward right top of present to highlight. Ribbons are Avocado. Pull Avocado Dip from top of ribbon down to highlight.
3. Use the background Sand color for your top present's base color. Diagonal stripes are Avocado Dip. Float shade left and bottom edges of package with Avocado. Float top and right edges with Cool White to highlight.
4. Holly: Base leaves with Avocado, float highlight with Avocado Dip. Line highlight on right edge with Cool White. Berries are dots of Cherry Red, highlighted with smaller dots of Cool White.
5. Bow: Line with Avocado. Line again more finely with Avocado Dip to highlight, then add some final highlights of Cool White. Knot is dotted with Avocado Dip, then highlighted with smaller dots of Cool White.

Cat
1. Background color is the base color of the cat. Base muzzle and tail with Cool White. Float shade cat with Neutral Grey (including around the outside of the cat on background). Float highlight cat with Cool White.
2. Nose is Fiery Red. Float shade left side of nose with Cherry Red. Dot upper right with Cool White to highlight.
3. Darken shading where mouth meets muzzle with a little Lamp Black.
4. Paint eyes with Cool White, iris with Avocado Dip + Avocado, and pupil with Lamp Black. Shade across the top of the eye with a narrow float of Lamp Black. Add two dots of Cool White in upper right and a fine crescent in lower left of each eye to highlight.
5. Stipple highlight in center of chest with Cool White.
6. Basecoat bow with Fiery Red. Float shade with Cherry Red, then deepen shading with Deep Burgundy.
7. Base tag on tail with Sand. Float top and right edges with Fiery Red to accent.
8. Finish cat by sketchily outlining and adding detail with a 00 permanent black pen.

Background
1. Float and drybrush some Avocado, Deep Burgundy, and Cherry here and there around edges to accent/frame the design. (I kept the floated red next to the green boxes, and green next to the red box.)

Pine Branch
1. Line branch with Avocado + Deep Burgundy.
2. Using a liner brush, pull needles with Avocado. Repeat with Avocado Dip. Finish by pulling some needles using a 00 permanent black pen to add a little definition.
3. Dot berries with Cherry Red. When dry, highlight with a smaller dot of Fiery Red.

Finishing
1. Review shading, highlights, and accents. Reinforce, if needed. Clean up any edges or details.
2. When using a permanent pen to line details, brushing varnish over it can sometimes have disastrous results because some inks will smear or bleed. To be safe, always set the ink by spraying with one or two light coats of a sealer/finisher. Let dry, then apply two or three coats of brush-on varnish.
3. Drill a hole at the top of each ornament, insert a piece of thin jute twine, and tie top into a bow to hang.

Techniques

Basecoating. Basecoat the design using as large a brush as possible for the area (normally a flat or angular for larger areas, and a round for small areas), and apply color as smoothly as possible. Don't worry if the basecoats aren't entirely even. After floating, drybrushing, and detailing, uneven basecoats will not be visible.

Brush mixing. Pick up one color and work it into the brush by blending on the palette. Pick up the second color and blend it in the same spot on the palette. If floating, blend the paint into the brush on the palette in the same manner as a normal float.

Floating. Float shading, highlighting, or accent colors using as large a flat or angular brush appropriate for the area (the larger the better). Saturate brush with water and touch against a paper towel to remove excess. Pick up color on the corner of the brush, then stroke firmly and repeatedly on the waxed palette to blend the color into the brush. Strong color on one corner should fade to clear water on the opposite corner.
Use short strokes to apply along the line to be shaded or highlighted, and then go back over in a continuous stroke to smooth. Too little water in the brush will cause the paint to skip and drag; too much water will cause it to puddle.

Drybrushing. Apply over basecoats to highlight, shade, or accent. Use a completely dry sable short round brush to pick up a little of the color and work it in a circular motion on the palette to blend the paint evenly into the brush. Brush off excess color onto a paper towel. Apply to the design area using a light touch, and work in a circular or crosshatching motion to blend the drybrushed color onto the surface. As more paint comes off your brush, it may be necessary to scrub a little harder, but this will help to softly blend the colors.

Stippling. Use a sable short round appropriate in size to the area. Pick up paint on the tip of the brush, and pounce up and down on the palette to distribute the color evenly through the bristles. Apply to the design using the same up and down pouncing motion. Pounce harder for more concentrated color and lighter for fading the color out.

Strengthening values. Drybrush or float an area two or three times to achieve the desired level of shading or highlighting. Keep the darkest values in the little triangular areas of the shadows.

Accents. Once painting is complete, go back and float or drybrush some colors from the palette into the shadows and edges of the design so the colors repeat throughout. This helps to avoid the cookie-cutter, pasted-on look.

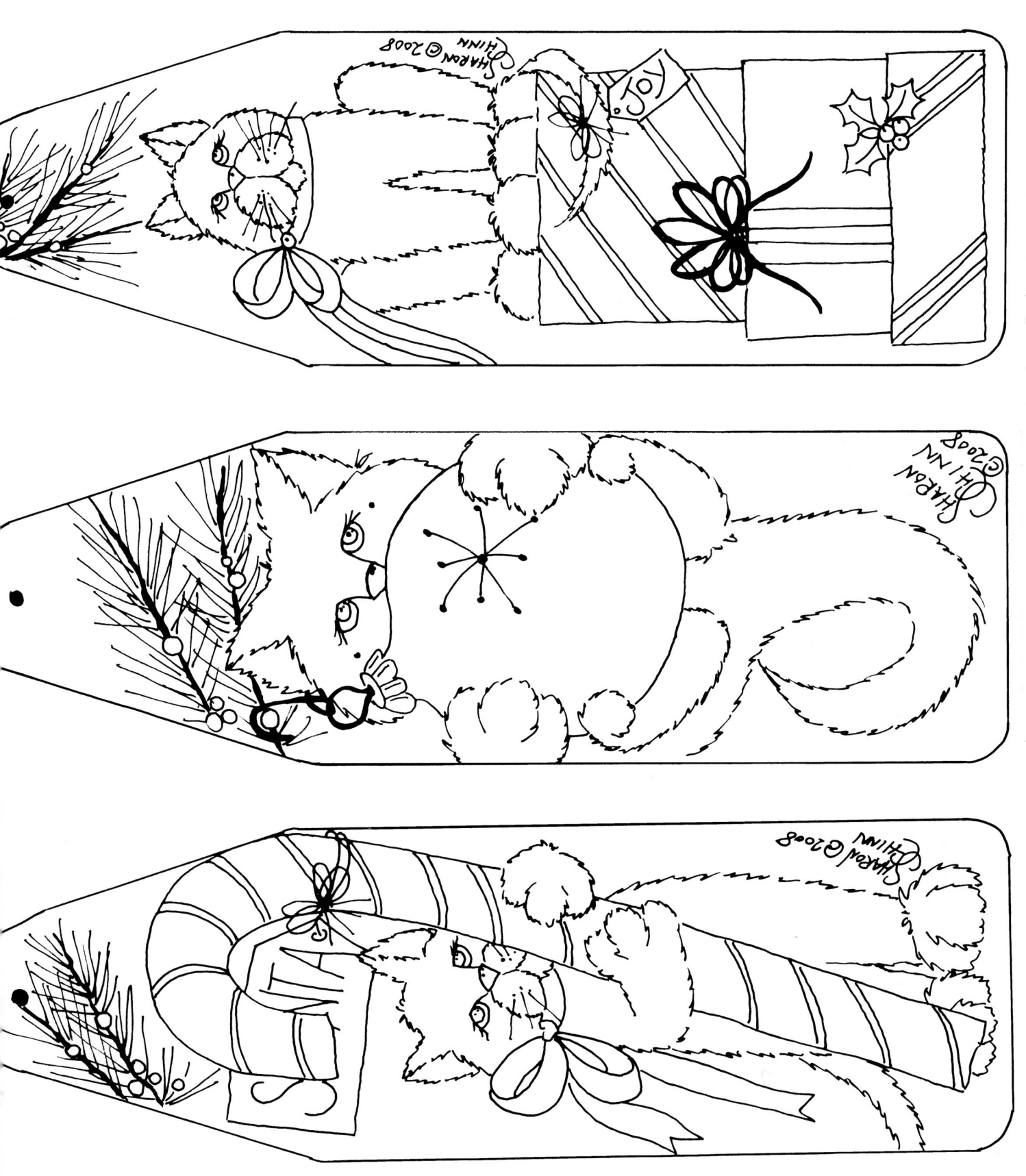

Christmas All Around

These big, cheerful ornaments will add color and sparkle to your Christmas tree. The festive Santa, angel, snowman, poinsettia, rose, and holly designs are also fun to paint on cards, boxes, tins, or practically any surface you'd like to decorate for the holidays. The colorful flower motif on the front of each ornament takes center stage on the back for a perfect finish.

Doxie Keller

Materials

SURFACE
Three 5½" papier maché discs available from Walnut Hollow (see resources, page 56)

PALETTE
DecoArt Americana Acrylics: Alizarin Crimson, Bleached Sand, Burnt Sienna, Cadmium Yellow, Hauser Dark Green, Kelly Green, Lamp Black, Olive Green, Mocha, Santa Red, Sea Aqua, Tangerine, White Wash, Williamsburg Blue

BRUSHES
Loew-Cornell, Inc.: ½" flat glaze (Series 798); #2, #6, #8 shader (Series 7300); #1 script liner (Series 800); #6, #8 (for cheeks) (Series FAB)

ADDITIONAL SUPPLIES
3" sponge roller, *DecoArt Patio Paint Outdoor Glitter, DecoArt Faux Glazing Medium, Identi-pen* (permanent black marker) or a double-ended *Sharpie Black Permanent Marker*

Note: Glazing is an easy way to shade and highlight. Work over a dry surface. Apply a thin coat of *Faux Glazing Medium.* Pick up paint on the corner of the brush and blend the color. Apply where you want either a shade or a highlight. Dry thoroughly between coats of glaze. You may apply up to four coats of glazing medium.

Preparation

1. Basecoat each disc with Bleached Sand, applying with a 3" sponge roller. This will give an eggshell texture. Two coats may be needed. Allow to dry.
2. Transfer patterns on pages 22–23 using gray transfer paper.

Painting

SANTA ORNAMENT

1. **Face:** Basecoat the face Mocha. Allow to dry then shade under the hat with Burnt Sienna. Dry rouge the cheeks and nose using the #6 FAB brush and Santa Red. Rub off excess paint using a circular motion. Fill in the mouth with Alizarin Crimson + a touch of Lamp Black. Lips are Santa Red with a White Wash highlight. Mustache is White with a Black outline. Eyes are outlined with the liner brush and Burnt Sienna. Using a stylus, place a white dot in each corner of the eye. Pupil is Williamsburg Blue with a shade of Black at the bottom. Place a white stylus dot in the upper right corner of the pupil around 1 o'clock.

2. **Hat:** Base in Santa Red. Allow to dry and paint Kelly Green stripes with the liner brush. Glaze and blend Black on the tassel section next to the front of the hat. Glaze White on the left front of the hat. This provides contrast between the two sections of the hat. For the fur on hat and tassel, dab on White Wash and shade by picking up a very small amount of Black; blend while wet on the left side of each. Work for texture.

3. **Beard:** Mix a light gray and follow the curve of the

beard with strokes of gray using the ½" brush or smaller. Allow to dry. Load the liner brush with White Wash and paint the curved lines of the beard allowing some of the gray to show through. When dry, outline all with the black fine-tip permanent pen. See photo for fly away whimsical hair outlines. When completely dry, brush on *Patio Paint Outdoor Glitter.*

4. **Poinsettias:** Use the Santa Red, Tangerine and Cadmium Yellow for contrast on the red leaves; shade the underneath leaves with Alizarin + a touch of Black or Kelly Green. Paint the layer of smaller leaves on top with touches of Tangerine and Cadmium Yellow. Use glazing medium for an easy application.

5. **Holly leaves and berries:** Fill in one side of each leaf with Olive Green and the other with Kelly Green. You could add touches of Williamsburg Blue or Cadmium Yellow. Outline with a black fine-tip pen when dry. Berries are large dots of Santa Red done with the wooden handle of a brush. Highlight with a glaze of white or pink (Santa Red + White).

6. Paint the background using glazing medium. Brush on a coat of glaze and pick up very small amounts of Williamsburg Blue then gently slip/slap the color on the background. Repeat with Santa Red, Cadmium Yellow, and Olive Green. This should be very pastel and blended one color into another (see photo).

7. Apply *Patio Paint Outdoor Glitter* to the beard, hat brim, pom-pom and poinsettia on the back of the ornament.

SNOWMAN ORNAMENT

1. **Body:** Using the #8 FAB brush, dab on the head and body of the snowman, shading each ball with a touch of Black and Williamsburg Blue.

2. **Face:** Dry rouge in the cheeks using the #6 FAB brush and Santa Red. Eyes and mouth are Black done with a script liner brush. Carrot nose is Tangerine shaded with Santa Red along the top and a touch of Cadmium Yellow on the end.

3. **Hat:** Paint Black and highlight on the left side with White Wash.

4. **Scarf:** Base in Santa Red. When dry, add Kelly Green stripes. Allow to dry then glaze the bottom side of the scarf sections with Black. Glaze the top of the sections with White. Fringe is Kelly Green outlined with the fine-tip black pen.

5. **Roses:** Paint the whole ball of the rose with Santa Red. Shade at the top of each ball with Alizarin Crimson. Shade the bottom with a glaze of Black. Add Cadmium Yellow stylus dots in the center of the top ball. Paint the comma strokes wrapping around the rose with the liner brush and a pink mix made from Santa Red + a touch of Alizarin + White.

6. See step 5 above for holly leaves and berries.

7. Paint background colors the same as for the Santa Ornament, step 6 above. I used more Williamsburg Blue and White plus a touch of Santa Red.

8. Allow all to dry thoroughly then outline with a black fine-tip permanent pen or the script liner and thinned Black paint.

9. **Snowflakes:** Outline with thinned Williamsburg Blue and place randomly. Apply *Patio Paint Outdoor Glitter* to the snowflakes, snow, snowman, and roses.

ANGEL ORNAMENT

1. **Face, hand, and legs:** Base in Mocha and glaze the face under the hair. Cheeks are dry rouged with Santa Red and the # 6 FAB brush. Use the fine-tip black pen for the eyes, nose, and mouth.

2. **Hair:** Tangerine outlined with the pen. Halo is a pale mix of Cadmium Yellow + a touch of Burnt Sienna. Allow to dry then add comma strokes with the liner brush and White Wash.

3. **Wings:** Cadmium Yellow. Shade the back wing with a glaze of Burnt Sienna. Glaze the top wing with a pale shade (use more glaze) of Burnt Sienna.

4. **Dress:** Base Williamsburg Blue then add Olive Green dots. When dry add Sea Aqua dots on top then loosely outline the circles with White. Sleeves are Olive Green. Add White commas at the sleeve bottom and dress neck.

5. **Holly leaves:** See step 5 of Santa Ornament.

6. **Flowers:** Use Santa Red, Tangerine, Alizarin, Crimson and White. Work quickly blending the colors while wet. You can refine with blending when the flowers are completely dry using the glazing technique to add touches of shades or highlights. Paint the centers using Cadmium Yellow and White, blending slightly.

7. See the Santa Ornament, step 6 above, for painting the background on both sides of the disc.

8. Outline with the black fine-tip pen or brush filled with thinned Black paint.

9. Cover about half of each flower with *Patio Paint Outdoor Glitter.*

ENLARGE PATTERNS 155%

The Tea Party

These tiny tea ornaments make perfect gifts for all of your tea loving friends! Practice the holiday roses a little before you begin, following the step-by-step page, then paint with joy!

Lynne Deptula

Materials

SURFACE
Porcelain ornaments, two tea pots and two tea cups, are available from Bows Plus (see resources, page 56)

PALETTE
DecoArt Americana Acrylics: Avocado, Black Plum, Burnt Umber, Electric Pink, Evergreen, Hauser Light Green, Lemonade, Midnite Green, Silver Sage Green, Tomato Red, True Red, Warm White

BRUSHES
Loew Cornell, Inc.: ¾" wash (Series 7150); #4, #8, #12 shaders (Series 7300); 18/0, #1, #6 liners (Series 7350)

ADDITIONAL SUPPLIES
DecoArt Americana Acrylic Sealer/Finisher, Matte

Preparation
1. Using the ¾" wash brush, basecoat the porcelain pieces with two thin coats of Silver Sage Green.
2. Transfer the patterns on page 26 or paint freehand.

Painting

HOLLY LEAVES
1. Using the #8 shader, basecoat the holly leaves with one layer of Avocado (see worksheet, page 27).
2. Shade the base of each leaf, breaking the shade to leave a thin vein line. Highlight just a tip or two of each leaf with a soft sideload float of Hauser Light Green.
3. Using the 18/0 liner and thinned Hauser Light Green, pull thin vein lines into each leaf. Loosely outline each leaf with a thin line of Avocado.

VINING AND BERRIES
1. Using a 18/0 liner and thinned Burnt Umber, pull loose vining lines onto the surface.
2. Along the vining on the Holiday Rose pieces, I used a stylus to dot the berries with Tomato Red. For the larger berries on the pine patterns, using a flattened #6 liner, paint various sizes and groups of berries casually along the vining.
3. Using the corner of a #4 shader sideloaded into Black Plum, shade the half of each berry which is closest to the vining. Highlight the opposite side with a sideload float of Electric Pink. This will probably look a little bright and chalky.
4. Thin True Red with water to a thin consistency and glaze all berries. Now they "glow" and look great! Highlight each berry with a very small dash or dot of Electric Pink using the 18/0 liner.

HOLIDAY ROSES
1. Using a #8 shader doubleloaded and well blended into Warm White and Silver Sage Green, stroke in the roses, starting with the back petals and keeping the Warm White side of the brush to the outside edge of each stroke.
2. Add the bowl, side petals and front petals to com-

plete the whole rose without rinsing and reloading the brush; keep picking up more Warm White on the highlight half of the brush for every stroke…lots of paint so that you really see each petal. Let the background work for you; it's a soft shade behind the rose petals!

PINE

1. Using a 18/0 liner and thinned paint, pull thin layers of the following colors to form each pine bough: Evergreen, Hauser Light Green, then a highlight layer of Lemonade needles. I like to pull each needle from the pine branch out to the tip…this way you will paint pointed and thin tipped needles.
2. The pine branches are painted as a line of Evergreen. I like to paint each individual pine bough wet into wet; it adds even more depth and variety of colors to the pine as the colors blend together.

TRIMS

1. Have fun with these! I used a #4 shader for the small Tomato Red or Avocado checker trims.
2. Paint the thin life lines, bow, strokes, and dashes with an 18/0 liner and Tomato Red.
3. For the plaid, flatten the #6 liner and use it as a small flat brush with Warm White to paint the plaid base then use the 18/0 liner to detail the plaid intersections with very thin Tomato Red dashes.
4. Paint the teacup knobs with Avocado.

Finishing

1. Erase any visible pattern lines.
2. Spray on two thin layers of *DecoArt Americana Acrylic Sealer/Finisher* in Matte.
3. Tie a gold cord or ribbon hanger to the handle of each ornament so they're ready for tree trimming.

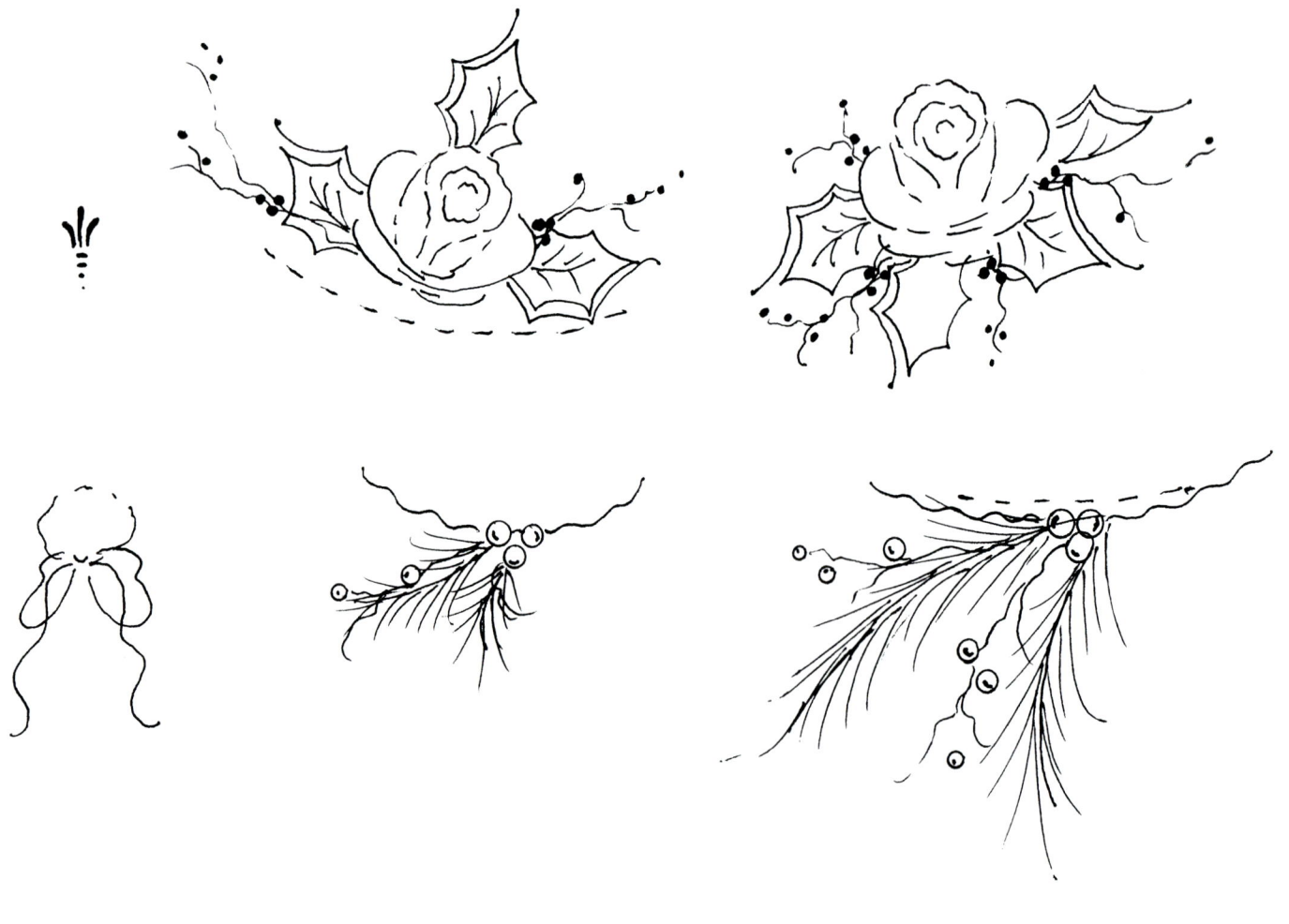

A Taste of Sweet

These puffed tin ornaments will bring back childhood memories of the simple joys of Christmas, like grandma's candy jar filled with gumdrops and garlands of wrapped peppermints decorating the tree. The festive treats are fun to paint and the finished ornaments make memorable gifts. But be sure to paint a set for yourself to sweeten your own tree.

Judy Diephouse

Materials

SURFACE
Puffed tin ornaments, heart, stocking, star, mitten, and plaque available from Della and Company (see resources, page 56)

PALETTE
Deco Art Americana Acrylics: Bright Green, Buttermilk, Cranberry Wine, Deep Midnight Blue, Hauser Dark Green, Holly Green, Honey Brown, Indian Turquoise, Mistletoe, Peony Pink, Primary Yellow, Sapphire Blue, Snow White, True Red, Yellow Light
DecoArt Hot Shots – Fiery Red

BRUSHES
Loew Cornell, Inc.: #4, #6, #8, #12 flats (Series 7300); 6/0, #1 liners (Series 7350); ¼" deerfoot (Series 7850)

ADDITIONAL SUPPLIES
Rust-oleum automobile primer, *DecoArt Americana Acrylic Sealer/Finisher, Gloss* spray, ⅛" red satin ribbon

Preparation

1. Spray the tin ornaments with automobile primer. Let dry thoroughly.
2. Sand lightly. Basecoat the ornaments with Buttermilk.
3. Transfer the patterns on pages 31–32.

Painting

STOCKING
1. Basecoat the cuff, toe, and heel with True Red.
2. Basecoat the cinnamon swirls with Cranberry Wine using a #6 flat. Using a 6/0 liner, starting at the center the swirl lines are Snow White. Using a #8 flat, shade the candy along the lower edge and in between the candies with a soft float of Deep Midnight Blue.
3. Using a #12 flat, sideload into Snow White. With the strongest color on the outside edge of the candy, float on a sheer wrapper. Using a 6/0 liner, add gather lines each way from the tie area with Snow White.
4. The ties are True Red, highlighted with a touch of *Hot Shots*–Fiery Red using a #1 liner.
5. Basecoat holly leaves Holly Green using a #4 flat. Using a #6 flat, shade the side of the leaves closest to the bottom of the ornament with Hauser Dark Green. Highlight the other side of the leaf with a float of Bright Green.
6. Using a 6/0 liner, the veins and outline on the light side are a brush mix of Bright Green and a touch of Primary Yellow.
7. Using a #1 liner, the additional strokes are Mistletoe.
8. Using a 6/0 liner, the plaid lines on the cuff, toe, and heel are Mistletoe, Bright Green, and White. The stitching by each of the sections is True Red.

HEART
1. Basecoat the nugget candy with Snow White using a #8 flat. Using a #1 liner, outline the candy with True Red then paint the tree shape in the middle with Mistletoe. Using a #8 flat, shade the candy with Deep Midnight Blue.
2. Using a #12 flat, float on the sheer wrapper with Snow White. The strongest color is along the outside edges. Add gather lines using a 6/0 liner.
3. Ties are True Red, highlighted with *Hot Shots*–Fiery Red.
4. Holly leaves and extra strokes are done the same as on the stocking.

5. Using a #1 liner, the "s" strokes along the edge are True Red with a dot of Mistletoe between.

STAR

1. Basecoat the candy canes with Snow White using a #6 flat. Using a #1 liner, the stripes are True Red.
2. Using a #8 flat, shade the lower side the candy canes with Deep Midnight Blue. Shade candy cane in the back with a soft float of Deep Midnight Blue. Using a #1 liner, add highlight shine lines with Snow White.
3. The ties around the candy canes are True Red, highlighted with Fiery Red.
4. The holly leaves and extra strokes are done the same as on the stocking.
5. Using a stylus add a dot border of True Red. Start at the point and dot along the edge letting the dots become smaller and smaller.

MITTEN

1. Basecoat the cuff with True Red.
2. Basecoat the peppermints with Snow White using a #8 flat. Shade the lower side and between the candies with a soft float of Deep Midnight Blue. Using a #1 liner, add shine lines of Snow White.
3. The holly leaves and extra strokes are done the same as on the stocking.
4. Using a #8 flat, the checks on the cuff are Snow White. Using a #1 liner, the trim line at the bottom of the cuff is Mistletoe.
5. Using a 6/0 liner, the stitching around the mitten is True Red.

PLAQUE

1. Basecoat the ¼" border around the edge with True Red. Using a #6 flat, basecoat one gumdrop True Red, one Primary Yellow, and one Sapphire Blue.
2. Shade the red gumdrop with Cranberry Wine; highlight with Peony Pink. Shade the yellow gumdrop with Honey Brown and highlight with Yellow Light and shade the blue gumdrop with Deep Midnight Blue and highlight with Indian Turquoise.
3. Using a ¼" deerfoot, lightly stipple the three gumdrops with Snow White. Using a fine stylus add a few more dots of White if needed.
4. Shade the red gumdrop with True Red and highlight with Fiery Red. Shade the yellow gumdrop with Primary Yellow and highlight with Yellow Light and shade the blue gumdrop with Sapphire Blue and highlight with Indian Turquoise.
5. Using a 6/0 liner, add a shine line of Snow White on each gumdrop.
6. The holly leaves and extra strokes are done the same as on the stocking.
7. Using a #1 liner, outline inside of the red border with Mistletoe.
8. Using the bigger end of the stylus, add dots of Snow White in the red border.

BACKS OF THE ORNAMENTS

1. Repeat the borders and trims on the backs of the ornaments to match the fronts.
2. Paint the holly leaves and extra strokes the same as on the stocking.
3. The berries are True Red, shaded with Cranberry Wine. Add a dot of Fiery Red for highlight.

Finishing

1. Allow the painting to dry thoroughly. Erase any visible transfer lines.
2. Spray several coats of *DecoArt Americana Acrylic Sealer/Finisher, Gloss*.
3. Cut five 12" pieces of ⅛" red satin ribbon for the decorative ribbon hangers for the ornaments. Tie to ornaments with a bow.

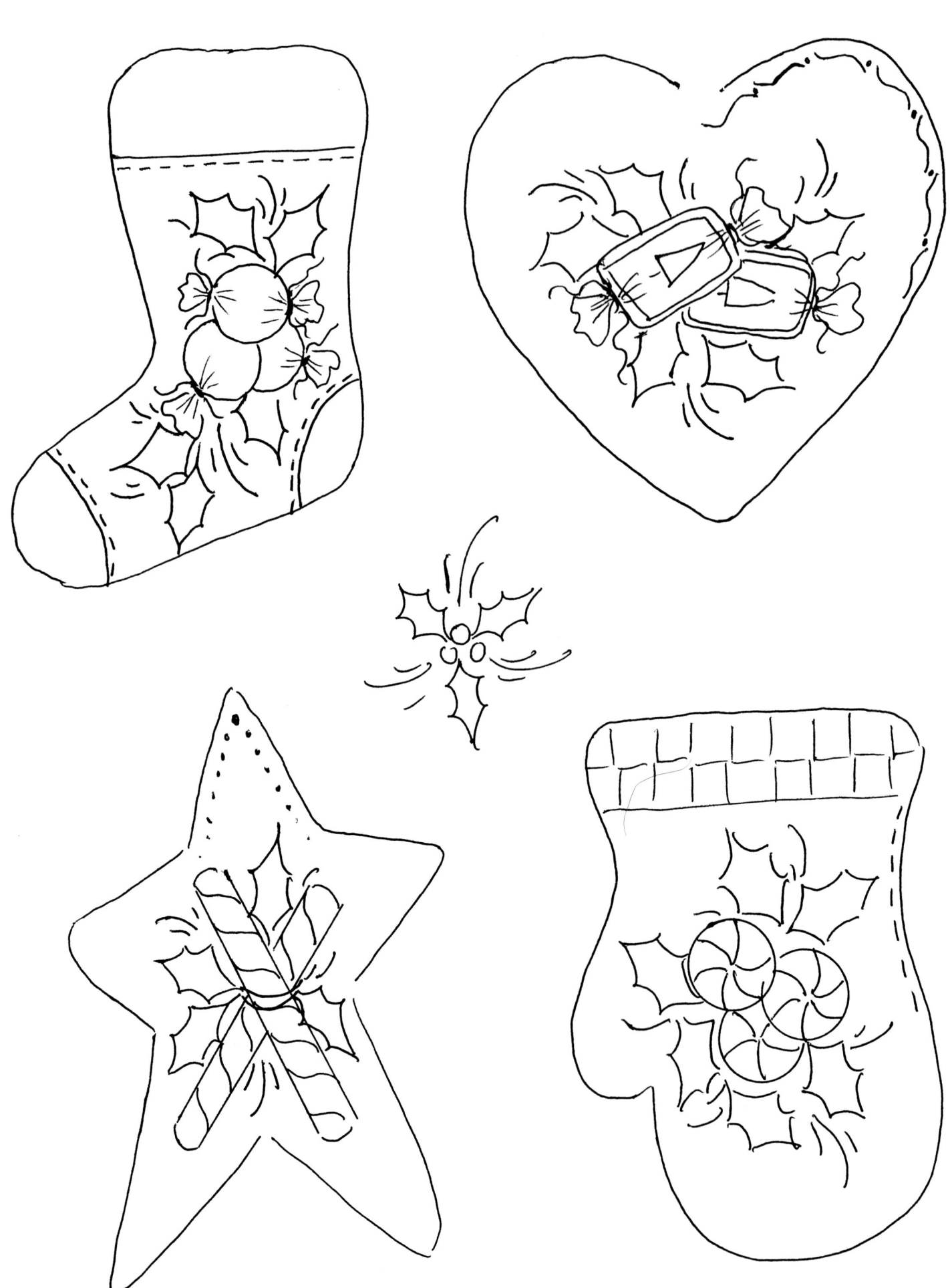

Winter Friends

These entertaining little characters are constant visitors to the feeder outside my window. So busy! Undaunted by winter chills, content with the provision of each day's blessings, confident the buds of spring are sleeping silently 'neath the crystal blankets of snow.

Lauré Paillex

Materials

SURFACE
Frosted glass ornaments by Krebs – 3¼ " dia., available from Hofcraft (see resources, page 56)

PALETTE
DecoArt Americana Acrylics: Blush Flesh, Burnt Umber, Gray Sky, Honey Brown, Lamp Black, Titanium White

BRUSHES
Loew-Cornell, Inc.: #8 flat (Series 7300); 10/0, #1 mid-liners (Series JS); #2, #4 filberts (Series 7500)

ADDITIONAL SUPPLIES
Lightweight tracing paper, extra-fine point drawing pen, #2 pencil, fine-point stylus, *DecoArt Star Lite Topcoat*, *DecoArt Paper Effects Dimensional Paintwriter* – Clear, *DecoArt Glamour Dust* – Crystal Glitter

Preparation

1. Mark a piece of lightweight tracing paper into several 3" squares, and copy one bird pattern on each using an extra-fine drawing pen.
2. Turn the paper over and retrace the lines on the reverse side using a #2 pencil. Cut the individual squares apart with scissors.
3. To transfer the patterns to the ornaments, position and hold a pattern, pencil lines down, against an ornament and carefully trace over the lines using a fine-point stylus.

Painting

1. Place the bird's eye with Lamp Black to accurately establish its location. Let dry.
2. Base the head and body with Gray Sky using a small filbert brush. Follow the natural contours of the body shape and keep your strokes lightly blended.
3. Place the cap and bib with a dark gray mix using equal parts Gray Sky + Lamp Black (1:1). A #1 liner or a small round brush works well for this step.
4. Stroke the long tail and wing feathers with Burnt Umber and dark gray loaded side-by-side (sideloaded) onto the #1 mid-liner. Note that feathers viewed from the underside of wings and tails are somewhat lighter in value.
5. Shade and detail the cap and bib with fine strokes of Lamp Black using a 10/0 liner. Float a shadow of thinned black onto the feathers at the base of the tail using a flat brush. Please refer to step 3 on the worksheet and note the placement of a floated shadow along the upper edge of the open wing also.
6. Apply a light overall layer of short feathery strokes to the face and breast using White and a #1 liner. Continue to build up a heavily textured application on the highlighted areas. Use a 10/0 liner to pull individual downy feather strokes around the edges as needed for detail.
7. Complete the details using the 10/0 liner brush. Re-paint the eye with black, then detail with a fine circle of gray around the inside edge and a tiny white highlight dot near an upper edge. Paint the beak and legs with dark gray and add highlights with Gray Sky. Use fine strokes of Gray Sky to define wing and tail feathers and to highlight the cap and bib.
8. Float a tint of Honey Brown along the underside of the wing, walking the thinned color downward towards the base of the tail (refer to step 4 on the worksheet). Let dry. Add a tint of Blush Flesh at the center of the dry Honey Brown float and also to the opposite edge of

the body near the leg. This final touch of color should be very subtle to produce a feeling of life and warmth.

9. Roughly stroke pine branches with Honey Brown and Burnt Umber loaded side-by-side onto a #1 liner brush (see illustration for details). Establish new growth at the bough tip with short strokes of Forest Green and Honey Brown. Paint the long pine needles with straight Forest Green. Add heavy drifts of snow along the branches and highlight several needles with White. Let dry completely.

Finishing

1. Apply a thin coat of *Star Lite Topcoat* (glitter varnish) to only the painted areas of the ornament—the bird and pine boughs. Allow varnish to dry completely.

2. For brilliant diamond-like sparkle and texture, accent the snow-laden branches and needles with *DecoArt Glamour Dust* dry crystal glitter using their *Clear Paper Effects* dimensional paintwriter as an adhesive. For best results, use the fine metal tip supplied with the product to control the placement of the paint/adhesive. While the adhesive is still wet, sprinkle on a generous amount of *Glamour Dust*, tapping and catching the excess glitter onto a sheet of paper so it may be channeled back into the bottle for re-use. Set the ornaments aside until the glitter application is completely dry. The Paper Effects paintwriter and *Glamour Dust* may also be used to personalize your ornament on the back side.

1. Base the eye Black. Place the head and body with Gray Sky.

2. Paint cap and bib with dark gray. Stroke tail and wing feathers with Burnt Umber and dark gray.

3. Build up White on face and breast. Shade and detail cap and bib with Black. Float Black at base of tail feathers and under open wing.

4. Add details to eye, beak, and legs. Apply tints of Honey Brown and Blush Flesh under wings.

1. Place rough branches with Honey Brown and Burnt Umber.

2. Stroke needles with Forest Green.

3. Add heavy White snow and highlights.

Jack-O'-Lantern Tree

Kids can get in on the fun by painting the jovial jack o' lantern ornaments for this delightful spider-topped Halloween tree. The pumpkin ornaments are made from recycled soda cans and are sure to become a Halloween tradition, whether they're decorating a table or hanging from a garland across the front porch.

Patricia Rawlinson

Materials

SURFACE
6¾" x 7¾" wood bowl, four 8 oz. emptied pop cans, two 14" thin dowels, wood chair leg, two wood bat cutouts, wood spider cutout with dowel holder, plastic spider. Kit available at www.patriciarawlinson.com (see resources, page 56)

PALETTE
DecoArt Americana Acrylics: Burnt Orange, Canyon Orange, Lamp Black, Primary Yellow

BRUSHES
Royal & Langnickel: XLG, medium crescent stencil Brush, #8 shader (Royal Fusion Series 3180), #1 liner (Royal Aqualon Series 2595), #2 round (Fusion Series 325), ½" oval wash (Aqualon Series 2950)

ADDITIONAL SUPPLIES
Automotive grey metal primer, fine black glitter, *Aleene's Clear Tacky Glue*, wire, felt pumpkin hats, hot glue gun, DecoArt Americana Satin Varnish

Preparation
1. Wash cans and allow to dry.
2. Spray with automotive metal primer.

Painting
1. Base the bowl, dowels, cans, and top and bottom sections of the chair leg with Burnt Orange using the oval wash. Apply enough coats for even coverage.
2. Base the spider, bats, and center section of the chair leg Lamp Black. Apply glue to the spider and sprinkle with black glitter.
3. Dip the "dry" XLG crescent stencil brush into the Canyon Orange paint and rub off onto a paper towel. Rub on the lightened areas of the project, repeating with Primary Yellow (this should happen gradually requiring several coats of the rubbing; switch dirty brush into the yellow color when ready). If you wash your brush you will need to allow it to dry before using again.
4. Using the smaller stencil brush, apply the highlights to the cans.
5. Transfer the patterns for the pumpkin faces (see page 40) and base the Pumpkin faces with the round brush using Lamp Black.
6. Transfer the pattern on the bowl and chair leg; line the pattern with thinned Lamp Black.
7. Apply dots using the back end of the appropriate sized brush. (Use fresh paint when applying dots.)
8. Use the #8 flat brush to make checks on the bowl.

Finishing
1. Varnish all the pieces except the spider. Use hot glue to adhere hats to top of cans and insert twisted wire hangers through holes in hat brims (see photo).
2. Screw the chair leg into the bowl, place the thin dowels through ¼" holes drilled in chair leg, insert dowel for spider into the top of the chair leg, and hot glue bats to top of chair leg.
3. Hang ornaments from your dowel tree and have a happy Halloween!

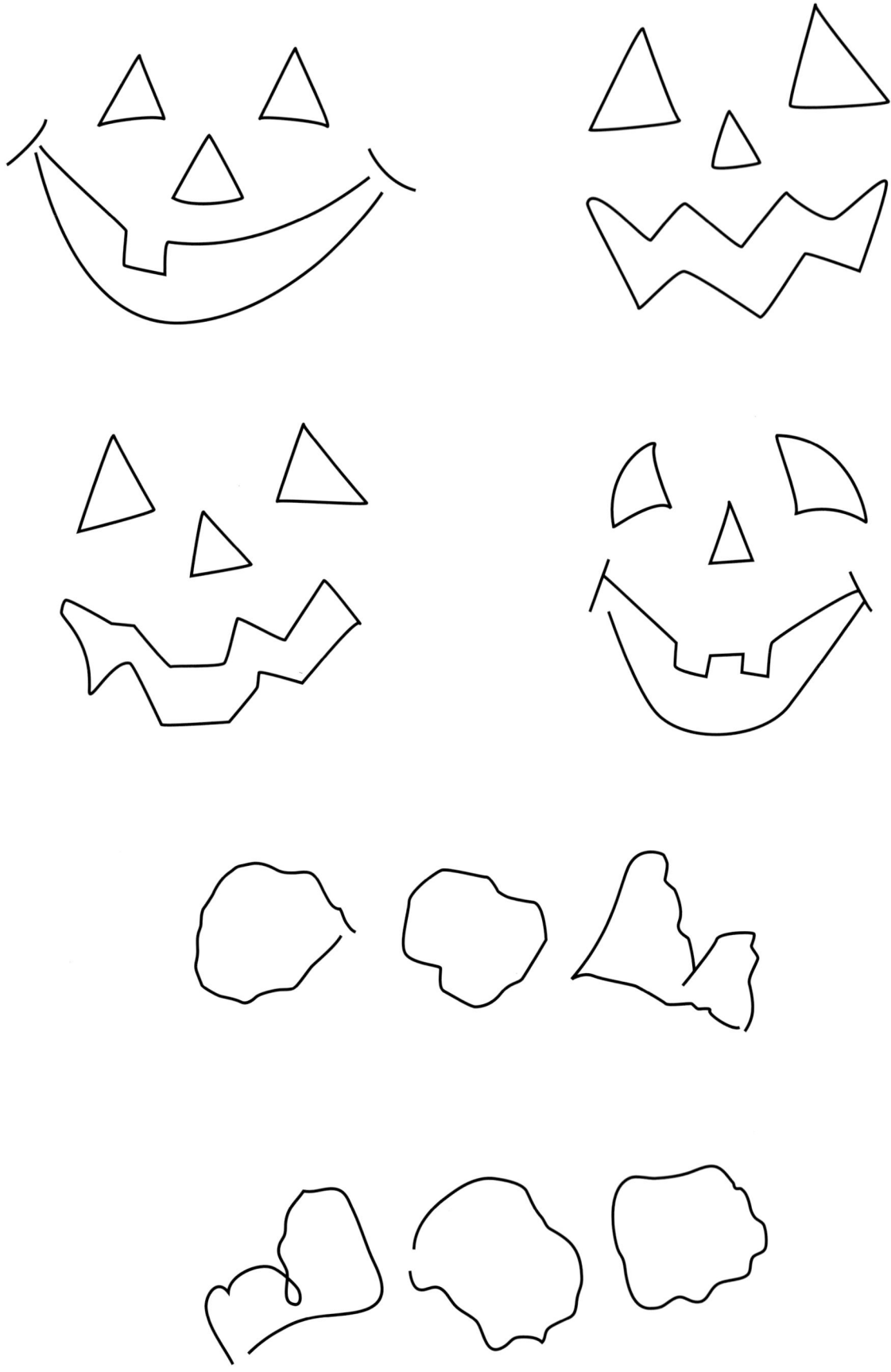

40

Tin Treasures

Bursting with holiday cheer, these folksy tin ornaments are also great little pockets for stashing holly sprigs, candy canes, gift cards, or other Christmas surprises. Filling them with goodies is sure to become a favorite holiday tradition.

Shara Reiner, CDA

Christmas Balls Pocket

Materials

SURFACE
Tin pocket, 4½" x 4½" excluding handle, available from Catalina Cottage (see resources, page 56)

PALETTE
DecoArt Americana Acrylics: Antique Rose, Black, Blue Mist, Cool Neutral, Country Red, Deep Burgundy, Deep Midnight Blue, Espresso, Foliage Green, Glorious Gold, Hauser Dark Green, Hauser Medium Green, Indian Turquoise, Spice Pink, Tangelo Orange, Warm White, Wedgewood Blue

BRUSHES
Loew-Cornell, Inc.: #8, #12, #16 shaders (Series 7300); #2 liner (Series 7350)

ADDITIONAL SUPPLIES
J.W. etc. Undercover, black permanent pen, matte spray, water-based varnish

Preparation
1. The tin comes ready to paint. Wipe to remove any dust.
2. Transfer the pattern on page 47 using light transfer paper.

Painting
1. Basecoat background Deep Midnight Blue.
2. Paint the ½" rim at the top with Warm White.

BALL #1
1. Basecoat Indian Turquoise. Shade the right side and across bottom with Wedgewood Blue and highlight the top with Indian Turquoise + Warm White.
2. Paint the stripe across the center with Foliage Green. Use the #8 shader brush and Antique Rose to paint the stripes. Shade the bottom of each stripe first with Country Red then with Deep Burgundy. Go back and shade each side of the center stripe with Wedgewood Blue.

BALL #2
1. Basecoat with Country Red. Shade the left side and across bottom with Deep Burgundy. Highlight the right side with Spice Pink.
2. Paint the strip across the center with Tangelo Orange. Highlight the right side with Tangelo Orange + Warm White.
3. Paint the dots Tangelo Orange. When dry add smaller dots of Tangelo Orange + Warm White.

BALL #3
1. Basecoat with Foliage Green. Shade the left side first with Hauser Medium Green then with Hauser Dark Green.
2. Paint polka dots Antique Rose. Shade the left side with Country Red then Deep Burgundy. Highlight the right side with Spice Pink.

HANGERS, BRANCHES, AND SNOWFLAKES
1. Basecoat all hangers with Cool Neutral. Shade the left side with Cool Neutral + Black.

2. Use the #2 liner and Espresso to paint the branches. Add strokes of Hauser Dark Green, Hauser Medium Green then Foliage Green for the pine needles. Paint berry dots first with Country Red, then add smaller dots with Antique Rose and Spice Pink as shown in photo.
3. Paint lines for snowflakes using the liner brush and Glorious Gold then add small dots at ends. Add Glorious Gold loops around branches for hangers.

TOP RIM
1. Paint stripes Country Red using the #8 shader. Shade stripes at the bottom with Deep Burgundy. Highlight each stripe with Spice Pink.
2. Line the left side of each stripe with Foliage Green.
3. Paint the raised wire trim with Glorious Gold.

Tobacco Can Angel

Materials

SURFACE
Tobacco can pocket, 3" x 4¼" excluding handle, available from Catalina Cottage (see resources, page 56)

PALETTE
DecoArt Americana Acrylics: Antique Rose, Black, Blue Haze Light, Burnt Sienna, Country Red, Deep Burgundy, Espresso, Fleshtone, Foliage Green, Glorious Gold, Hauser Medium Green, Indian Turquoise, Spice Pink, Tangelo Orange, Warm White, Wedgewood Blue, Yellow Ochre

BRUSHES
Refer to Christmas Balls Pocket above.

ADDITIONAL SUPPLIES
Papier maché heart from local craft store, black permanent pen

Preparation
1. The tin comes ready to paint. Wipe to remove dust.
2. Transfer the pattern on page 46 using light transfer paper.

Painting
1. Basecoat with Blue Haze Light. Paint trim at the top with Warm White.
2. Paint the angel's face Fleshtone; shade outside edges with Fleshtone + Burnt Sienna. Use the #2 liner and Fleshtone + Burnt Sienna to paint the nose. Use a wash of Antique Rose for the cheeks. The eyes are Black and hair is Tangelo Orange. Paint the halo Indian Turquoise.
3. Paint the wings Warm White. Paint the dress Deep Burgundy then drybrush with Country Red and Antique Rose. Add buttons under the neck with Spice Pink and the bow with Black.
4. Her arms are Country Red + a tad of Antique Rose.
5. Paint the star Yellow Ochre; add a dot to the end of each point. Paint the Candy Cane Warm White; stripe with Country Red and shade the inside edge with Wedgewood Blue. Paint the hand Fleshtone.
6. Paint the tree trunk with Espresso and the pine boughs using the liner and Hauser Medium Green and Foliage Green. Paint the treetop star with True Ochre.
7. Paint stripes on the top trim using Country Red and shade at the bottom with Deep Burgundy. Line the left side of each stripe with Hauser Medium Green. Add gold trim around edges with Glorious Gold. Also add gold trim around the bottom of the can.
8. Add double wiggly lines around the star and wings and outline some tree boughs using a Black permanent pen.

Stocking Pockets

Materials

SURFACE
Tin stocking pockets, 2¼" x 7½", available from Della & Company (see resources, page 56)

PALETTE
DecoArt Americana Acrylics: Antique Rose, Black, Blue Haze, Blue Mist, Country Red, Deep Burgundy, Foliage Green, Hauser Dark Green, Hauser Medium Green, Reindeer Moss Green, Spice Pink, Warm White

BRUSHES
Refer to Christmas Balls Pocket above.

ADDITIONAL SUPPLIES
J.W. etc. UnderCover, matte spray, water-based varnish

Preparation
1. Apply two coats of *J.W. etc. UnderCover* to tin pieces. Let dry overnight.
2. Transfer the patterns on page 46 using grey transfer paper.

Painting

BLUE STOCKING

1. Basecoat with Blue Mist. Paint the cuff Warm White. When dry add Black checks.
2. Paint the toe patch Reindeer Moss Green with Hauser Medium Green stripes. Paint the heel patch Spice Pink; add Country Red plaid pattern and dot where plaid crosses with Deep Burgundy. Paint the heart patch Antique Rose. Shade the point with Country Red then Deep Burgundy. Highlight the fat parts with Spice Pink.
3. Paint background stripes with Blue Mist + Warm White. Shade under the cuff with Blue Haze.
4. Use a Black permanent pen to add spirals and outlines to cuff and stitching around patches.

HOLLY STOCKING

1. Basecoat Reindeer Moss Green. Paint the 1/2" band at the top and the heel patch Warm White. Paint the toe patch Blue Mist. Add country Red stripes on the band using the #6 shader. Shade bottom of each stripe with Deep Burgundy and highlight top with Spice Pink.
2. Paint holly leaves Hauser Medium Green; shade with Hauser Dark Green and highlight with Foliage Green. Paint berries Country Red; shade with Deep Burgundy and highlight with Spice Pink.
3. Shade under the cuff with Hauser Dark Green. Paint the toe patch stripes with Warm White and the heel patch checks with Black.
4. Add background dots with Warm White.
5. Add stitching lines around patches and double wiggly lines around holly and cuff using a Black permanent pen.

Finishing

1. Spray with matte spray to set the ink.
2. Varnish with 2–3 coats of water-based varnish.

Candy Cane and More

Materials

SURFACE

Hanging tin, 4" x 6½", available from Della & Company (see resources, page 56)

PALETTE

DecoArt Americana Acrylics: Antique Rose, Black, Blue Mist, Country Red, Deep Burgundy, Deep Midnight Blue, Espresso, Foliage Green, Hauser Medium Green, Spa Blue, Spice Pink, Warm White, Yellow Ochre

BRUSHES

Refer to Christmas Balls Pocket above.

ADDITIONAL SUPPLIES

J.W. etc. UnderCover, bi amlack permanent pen

Preparation

1. Apply two coats of *J.W. etc. UnderCover* and let dry overnight.
2. Transfer the pattern on page 47 using grey transfer paper.

Painting

1. Basecoat with Blue Mist. Wash both ball ornaments with Warm White. Paint the candy cane Warm White and the star Yellow Ochre.
2. Paint stripes on the left ornament Warm White then add Country Red stripes. Shade the ornament with Deep Midnight Blue. Add Warm White dots. Paint the grey hanger with Black + Warm White. Shade the outside edges with a darker mix and highlight the center with a lighter mix of the same colors.
3. Paint the stripe on the right ornament with Foliage Green. Shade the outside edges with Hauser Medium Green and highlight the center with Foliage Green + Warm White. Shade the ball including the band with Deep Midnight Blue. Paint the stars Warm White and the dots on the band Spice Pink.
4. Shade the left side of the star with Deep Burgundy and highlight the right side with Yellow Ochre + Warm White.
5. Paint the candy cane stripes Antique Rose. Shade the inside edge with Country Red then with Deep Burgundy. Highlight the outside edge with Spice Pink. Shade the inside edge of the Warm White with Deep Midnight Blue. Highlight each red stripe with a line of Warm White near the outside edge. Paint the bow Hauser Medium Green and highlight with Foliage Green.
6. Paint branches with Espresso. Add pine needles using Hauser Medium Green and Foliage Green. Add dots of Country Red for the berries then highlight with Spice Pink.
7. The trim line around the outside edge is Spa Blue.
8. Use a Black permanent pen to add the wire hanging loops and bows and to outline the pine boughs as shown.

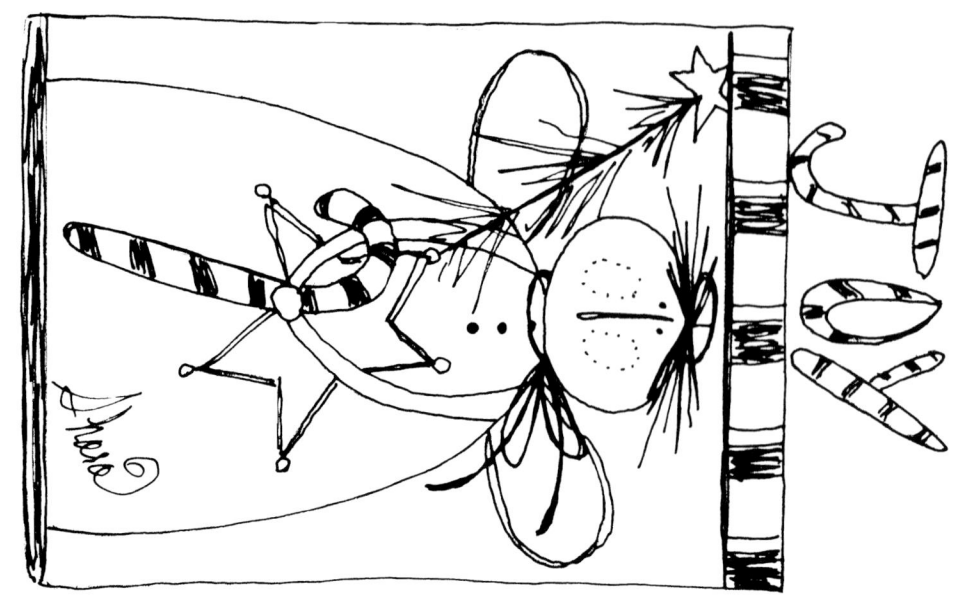

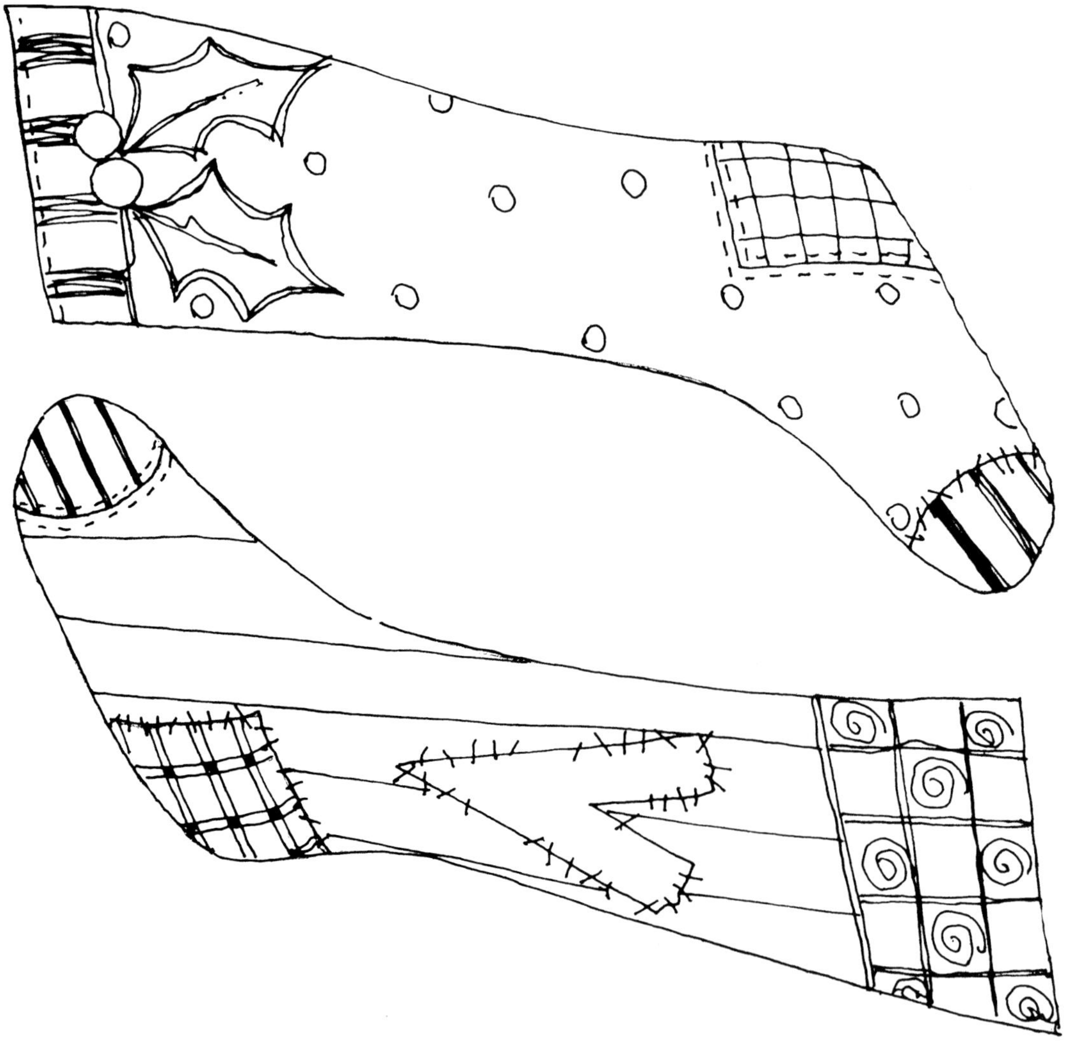

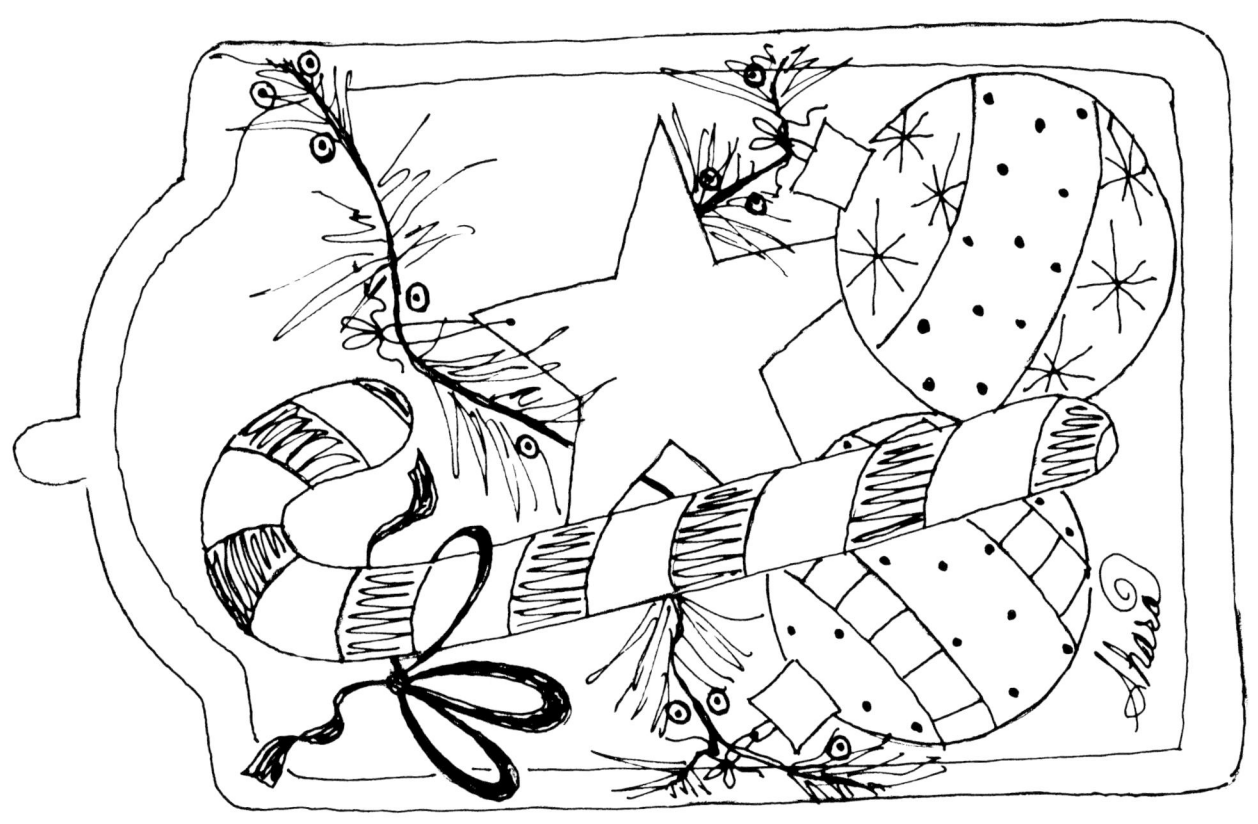
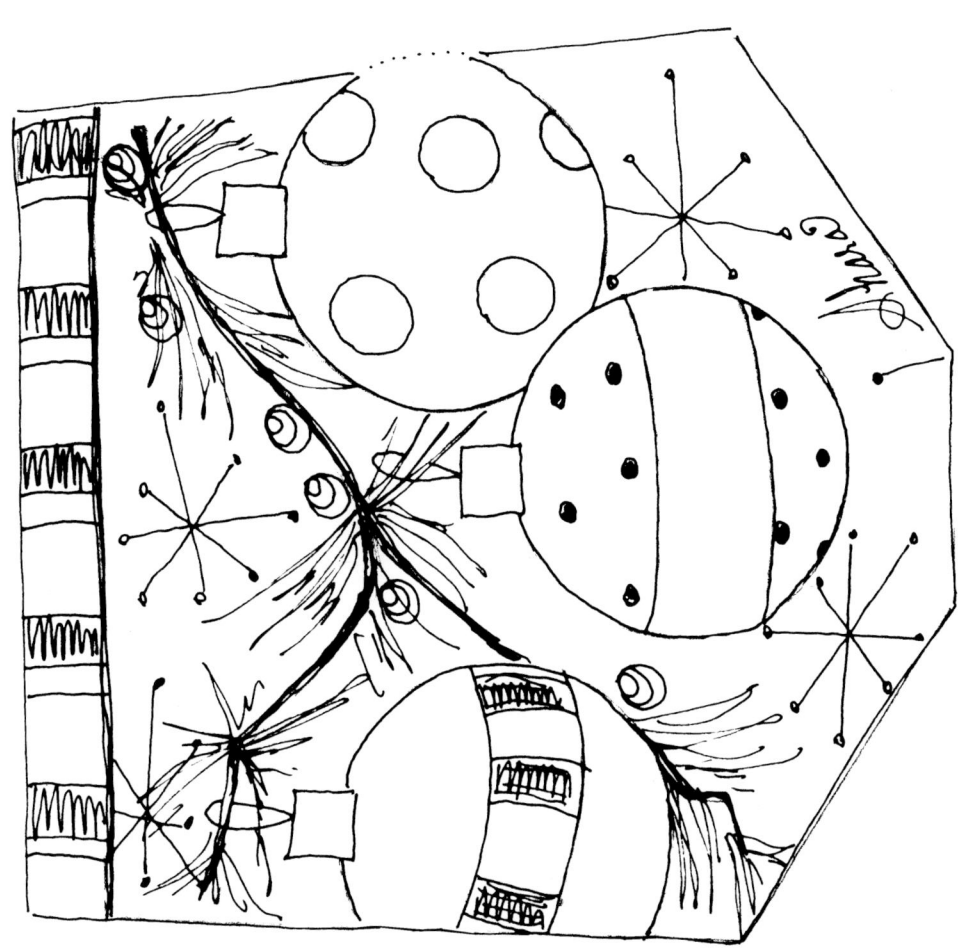

Spring Floral Eggs

Reminiscent of beautiful Chinese cloisonné, these floral egg ornaments will add artistic elegance to your springtime decorating. Outline the classic flowers with metallic gold and enhance with sparkly rhinestones for jewel-like grandeur, then display singly on stands or hang a grouping on a decorative tree branch.

Chris Thornton-Deason

Materials

SURFACES
Two large eggs 4", one egg 3"; stands of choice available from local craft store

PALETTE
DecoArt Americana Acrylics: Avocado Dip, Petal Pink, Plantation Pine, Glorious Gold, Grape Juice, Warm White, Wisteria

BRUSHES
Loew-Cornell La-Corneille Golden Taklon: 1" glaze (Series 7350); #4, #8, #10 shaders (Series 7300); #1 script liner (Series 7050)

ADDITIONAL SUPPLIES
Sandpaper 250-300 grit, *DecoArt Mutli-Purpose Sealer; Delta Creative Stencil Mania Décor Accents, DecoArt DuraClear Satin Varnish,* craft glue, crystal rhinestones

Preparation

1. Always sand with the grain of the wood. Using fine grit sandpaper, sand off burrs and rough edges from the frame; remove dust.
2. Apply one even coat of multi-purpose sealer to each egg using the 1" wash brush. Allow to dry thoroughly.
3. Sand with fine grit sandpaper. Remove dust.

Painting

HYDRANGEA EGG
1. Basecoat the entire egg using the 1" wash brush in a doubleload of Wisteria and Grape Juice; use a slip/slap motion, lightly blending the colors.
2. Apply the pattern for petals on page 50 if desired. These are random and can easily be freehanded.
3. Using the #8 shader, float all of the Wisteria petals.
4. Repeat the process floating all of the pink petals in a mix of equal parts Petal Pink + Wisteria.
5. Float the shadows on each petal in the center of all of the flowers in Grape Juice using the #8 shader.
6. Reinforce the highlights with a float of Warm White + a touch of Petal Pink or Wisteria randomly here and there.
7. Stroke the leaves in a doubleload of Avocado Dip and Plantation Pine using the #10 shader.
8. If desired, add the fleur de lis using the stencil from the *Stencil Mania Décor Accents*. Stencil the background with Glorious Gold then outline with Grape Juice.

NARCISSUS EGG
1. Basecoat the entire egg using the 1" wash brush in a doubleload of Wisteria and Petal Pink; use a slip/slap motion, lightly blending the colors.
2. Apply the pattern repeating four times around the egg.
3. Basecoat the back petals of the flower in Warm White + a touch of Avocado Dip using the #10 shader.
4. Using the same brush, float the shadows dividing the petals and around the center in Avocado Dip.
5. Reinforce the deeper shadows with a float of Plantation Pine using the same brush.
6. Float the highlights with Warm White using the #8 shader.
7. Basecoat the centers of the flowers in a mix of equal parts Petal Pink + Warm White + Wisteria using the #8 shader.
8. Float the shadows under the ruffle, across the

bottom of the bowl and inside the bowl in Petal Pink + a touch of Grape Juice using the #8 shader.

9. Reinforce the shadows by adding a touch more Grape Juice using the same brush.

10. Float the highlights on the ruffle in Warm White + a touch of Petal Pink using the #8 shader.

11. Stroke the leaves in a doubleload of Avocado Dip and Plantation Pine using the #10 shader.

12. If desired, add the fleur de lis using the stencil from the *Stencil Mania Décor Accents*. Stencil the background with Glorious Gold then outline with Grape Juice.

LILY OF THE VALLEY

1. Basecoat the entire egg using the 1" wash brush in a doubleload of Wisteria and Grape Juice; use a slip/slap motion, lightly blending the colors.

2. Apply the pattern repeating three times around the egg.

3. Basecoat the leaves in a mix of equal parts Plantation Pine + Avocado Dip using the #10 shader; also do the stems in this color using the #1 liner.

4. Float the shadows through the center and across the bottom in Plantation Pine using the #10 shader.

5. Float the highlights across the top and down through the center in Avocado Dip using the #8 shader.

6. Reinforce the highlights with Warm White + a touch of Avocado Dip using the same brush.

7. Basecoat the flowers in Warm White + a touch of Avocado Dip using the #4 shader.

8. Float the shadows across the top of the flower in Avocado Dip using the same brush; float the highlights across the bottom in Warm White.

9. If desired, add the fleur de lis using the stencil from the *Stencil Mania Décor Accents*. Stencil the background with Glorious Gold then outline with Grape Juice.

Finishing

1. Do all gold linework including the stamens of the narcissus and the centers of the hydrangeas using the #1 liner and Glorious Gold.

2. Apply as many coats of satin varnish as desired using the 1" wash brush.

3. Glue all rhinestones in place.

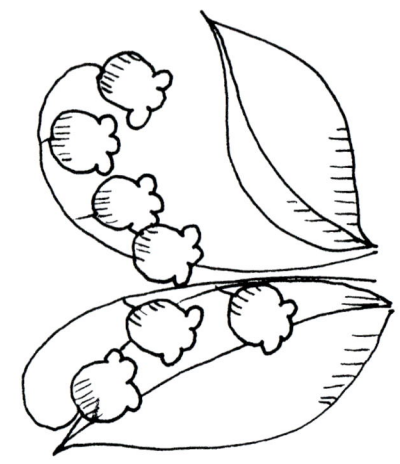

Yuletide Favorites

Seasonal favorites, santa, snowmen, and holly, will add traditional charm to your Christmas tree. Liquid Shadow gives added dimension to the turned wood ornaments for perfect antiquing without floating colors.

MaryJo Tuttle

Materials

SURFACE
Wooden Teardrop A Ornament – #101137; Wooden Victorian B Ornament – #101138; Wooden Victorian C Ornament – #101139 available from Cabin Crafters (see resources, page 56)

PALETTE
DecoArt Americana Acrylics: Antique Rose, Antique White, Avocado, Avocado Dip, Burnt Orange, Camel, Deep Midnight Blue, Espresso, French Grey Blue, Graphite, Hauser Dark Green, Honey Brown, Lamp Black, Light Avocado, Light Mocha, Medium Flesh, Milk Chocolate, Neutral Grey, Payne's Grey, Rookwood Red, Shading Flesh, Snow White, Tuscan Red
Hot Shots – Fiery Red, *Dazzling Metallics* – Emperor's Gold

ADDITIONAL SUPPLIES
Kerry Trout's Liquid Shadow (available from the Artist's Club), DecoArt MultiPurpose Sealer, DecoArt Spray Sealer/Finisher – Matte, ribbon for hanging

BRUSHES
The Artist's Club Papillon: #4, #8 shaders; 5/8" angular shader; 3/4" glaze wash; 1/8" filbert comb; Stipple Set, Midliner Set, Highlighter Set

Preparation

1. Sand and seal the ornaments with multipurpose sealer. When dry, sand again and remove sanding dust with a damp paper towel.
2. Basecoat the ornaments as follows, transferring the patterns on page 55 as needed:

Holly Ornament (Victorian C):
- Emperor's Gold – top
- Rookwood Red – section under top and large section at the bottom (dots, Emperor's Gold)
- Antique White – checked areas (checks, Lamp Black) and center design area
- Avocado – remaining sections
- Light Avocado – Holly Leaves

Santa Ornament (Teardrop A):
- Emperor's Gold – top
- Antique White – checked areas (checks, Lamp Black)
- Camel – oval
- Deep Midnight Blue – stripe around oval
- Avocado – body of ornament around oval
- Rookwood Red – bottom section (dots, Emperor's Gold), Santa's hat & coat
- Medium Flesh – Santa's Face
- Neutral Grey – Santa's hair, beard, and mustache
- Milk Chocolate – stipple hat cuff and ball
- Espresso – branches

Snowman Ornament (Victorian B):
- Emperor's Gold – top
- Antique White – checked areas (checks, Lamp Black)
- Deep Midnight Blue – large design area
- Rookwood Red – bottom section (dots, Emperor's Gold)
- Light Mocha – stipple man faces
- Neutral Grey – undercoat all snowman hats
- Snowman A – Light Avocado – brim; Camel – hat (X's, Light Avocado)
- Snowman B – Rookwood Red – brim and ball; French Grey Blue – hat (stripes, Light Mocha and Tuscan Red)
- Snowman C – Antique Rose – brim; Light Avocado – hat
- Snowman D – Honey Brown – brim and ball (stripes, Light Mocha and Avocado); Tuscan Red – hat
- Snow White – line the flakes

Painting

HOLLY ORNAMENT

1. Shade the bottom of the top red section and top and bottom of the bottom red section with *Liquid Shadow*. Highlight with *Hot Shots* – Fiery Red. Shade the bottom

of the top green section and top of the bottom green section with Hauser Dark Green. Highlight with Avocado Dip. Shade the top of the light checks on all sections with Milk Chocolate. Shade the top and bottom and around the holly leaves on the main section with Milk Chocolate. Highlight the open areas around the design with a drybrush of Light Mocha.

2. Shade the base and along the vein lines of all leaves with Hauser Dark Green. Highlight the tips of all leaves and opposite side of the vein lines with Avocado Dip. Outline and stitch the vein lines with Lamp Black. The berries are brush end dots of Tuscan Red. When dry, shade the sides closest to the leaves with *Liquid Shadow* and highlight the other with *Hot Shots* – Fiery Red. Add dot highlights of Snow White to the highlighted sides. Add vines with Hauser Dark Green.

SANTA ORNAMENT

1. Shade the top of the light checks on both sections with Milk Chocolate. Shade the top of the red section with *Liquid Shadow* and highlight with *Hot Shots* – Fiery Red. Shade around the top and bottom, around the oval and under the branches on the green section with Hauser Dark Green. Shade around the inside of the oval with Honey Brown. Stitch around the inside of the blue stripe, and add a wavy line around the outside of the blue stripe and top and bottom of the checked sections with Emperor's Gold.

2. Shade Santa's face under the hat and above the nose with Shading Flesh. Blush the cheeks and bottom of the nose with Antique Rose. Highlight the eye area and top of the nose with Light Mocha. The eyes are Lamp Black; the eyebrows are Light Mocha. Add dot highlights to the upper right of the eyes and top of the cheeks with Snow White. Stroke in the hair and beard, using the $1/8$" filbert comb and line the mustache with Light Mocha. Go over these areas again using Snow White. Shade the hair under the hat, the middle of the mustache and under the mustache with Graphite. With your liner brush, add some more hairs to break up the shade lines.

3. Shade Santa's hat above the brim, in the fold, both sides of the tail, and on his coat under the beard with *Liquid Shadow*. Highlight the center areas of the hat and coat with *Hot Shots* – Fiery Red. Stipple the cuff and ball with Honey Brown and then Camel. Shade both sides of the cuff and top of the ball with Espresso. Stipple a little Light Mocha in the center of the cuff and bottom of the ball to highlight. Outline as necessary with Lamp Black.

4. Add the needles to the branches with Hauser Dark Green, Light Avocado, and Light Mocha. Add the snow to the branches with Snow White.

SNOWMAN ORNAMENT

1. Shade the top of the light checks on both sections with Milk Chocolate. Shade the top of the red section with *Liquid Shadow* and highlight with *Hot Shots* – Fiery Red. Shade the top and bottom of the design section with Payne's Grey. With French Grey Blue, float around each snowman.

2. Shade all snowman faces under the hat and slightly down each side with Deep Midnight Blue. Highlight the center of the faces by stippling with Snow White. Blush the cheeks with Antique Rose. Base the noses with Burnt Orange, shade at the base with Rookwood Red, and highlight at the tip with *Hot Shots* – Fiery Red. The eyes and mouth lines are Lamp Black. Highlight the eyes and top of the cheeks with small dots of Snow White.

3. Snowman A: Shade the sections of the brim with Hauser Dark Green and highlight with Avocado Dip. Shade the hat against the brim with Honey Brown. Stipple the ball with Hauser Dark Green, Avocado Dip, and Light Mocha.

4. Snowman B: Shade both sides of the brim and bottom of the ball with *Liquid Shadow*. Highlight the center of the brim and top of the ball with *Hot Shots* – Fiery Red. Shade both sides of the hat with Deep Midnight Blue and highlight the center with Light Mocha. Line the star on the brim with Snow White.

5. Snowman C: Shade both sides of the brim with Rookwood Red and highlight the center with *Hot Shots* – Fiery Red. Highlight the top of the hat with Avocado Dip. The lines on the hat are Tuscan Red. Shade the hat against the brim with Hauser Dark Green. Line the pom-pom with Snow White.

6. Snowman D: Shade both sides of the brim and top of the ball with Rookwood Red and highlight the center of the brim and bottom of the ball with Camel. Shade the hat against the brim, under the fold, and both sides with *Liquid Shadow*. Highlight the center of the hat with *Hot Shots* – Fiery Red.

7. Outline the snowmen as necessary with Lamp Black.

8. Dot the flakes and add dots to the design area with Snow White.

Finishing

1. Finish the ornaments with several coats of *DecoArt Spray Sealer/Finisher* – Matte.

2. Add a ribbon hanger and enjoy!

ENLARGE PATTERNS 125%

55

Resources

Artist's Club
P.O. Box 8930
Vancouver, WA 98668-8930
800-845-6507
www.artistsclub.com

Bows Plus Bisque
24 Augusta Way
N. Chelmsford, MA 01863
978-251-0111
www.bowsplusbisque.com

Catalina Cottage
65 Brea Canyon #C
Walnut, CA 91789
909-598-4200
866-848-TOLE (orders only)
www.catalinacottage.com

Cabin Crafters
1225 W. 1st St.
P.O. Box 270
Nevada, IA 50201
800-669-3920
www.cabincrafters.com

DecoArt Inc.
P.O. Box 386
Stanford, KY 40484
800-477-8478
www.decoart.com

Della and Company
Della Wetterman
5208 Lake Charles
Waco, TX 76710
254-772-6927
www.DellaAndCompany.com

Delta Ceramcoat
2690 Pellissier Pl.
City of Industry, CA 90601
800-423-4135
www.deltacrafts.com

Hofcraft
P.O. Box 72
Grand Haven, MI 49417
800-828-0359
www.hofcraft.com

J.W. etc.
1212 N Tancahua St.
Corpus Christi, TX 78401
361-887-6600
www.jwetc.com

Loew-Cornell, Inc.
400 Sylvan Ave.
Englewood Cliffs, NJ 07632
201-836-7070
www.loew-cornell.com

Royal & Langnickel
6707 Broadway
Merrillville, IN 46410
800-247-2211
www.royalbrush.com

Sweet Patoodies
726 Meadowview Drive
Villa Hills, KY 41017
859-341-3533
www.sweetpatoodies.com

Walnut Hollow
1409 State Road 23
Dodgeville, WI 53533
800-950-5101
www.walnuthollow.com

Artists

Jane Allen
210 Garrett Lane
Camp Hill, PA 17011
717-737-1801
alandjanie@msn.com

Sharon Chinn, CDA
Sweet Patoodies
726 Meadowview Drive
Villa Hills, KY 41017
859-341-3533
sharon@sweetpatoodies.com
www.sweetpatoodies.com

Lynne Deptula
Distinctive Brushstrokes
7245 Cascade Woods Dr. SE
Grand Rapids, MI 49546
616-940-1899
Dbrush@aol.com
www.distinctivebrushstrokes.com

Judy Diephouse
Distinctive Brushstrokes
9796 Myers Lake Ave.
Rockford, MI 49341
616-874-1656
distinctj@aol.com
www.distinctivebrushstrokes.com

Linda Gillum
Kooler Design Studio
399 Taylor Blvd. Ste. 104
Pleasant Hill, CA 94523
925-689-0801
Lindajgillum@aol.com
www.koolerdesign.com

Doxie Keller
127 West 30th Ave.
Hutchinson, KS, 67502
620-665-6256
doxie@southwind.net

Lauré Paillex
P.O. Box 1495
Buzzards Bay, MA 02532-1495
508-579-4623
laureart@comcast.net
www.laureart.com

Patricia Rawlinson
P.O. Box 938
Gallipolis, OH 45631
503-504-5561
www.patriciarawlinson.com

Shara Reiner, CDA
Angel Thyme Designs
12815 Camino De La Breccia
San Diego, CA 92128
858-395-7588
angelthyme@san.rr.com

Chris Thornton-Deason
P.O. Box 617
Douglass, KS 67039
316-253-5442
cricinda@earthlink.net
www.ChrisThorntonDesigns.com

MaryJo Tuttle
Tuttle's Touches
4300 Washington St.
Vancouver, WA 98660
360-693-1938
www.tuttlestouches.com

Produced by:

Kooler Design Studio, Inc.
399 Taylor Blvd., Suite 104
Pleasant Hill, CA 94523
info@koolerdesign.com

Production Team:
- Creative Director: Donna Kooler
- Editor-In-Chief: Judy Swager
- Art Director: Basha Kooler
- Senior Graphic Designer: Ashley Rocha
- Photographer: Dianne Woods

Published by:

Copyright ©2009 by Leisure Arts, Inc.,
5701 Ranch Drive, Little Rock, AR 72223
www.leisurearts.com

We have made every effort to ensure that these instructions are accurate and complete. We cannot, however, be responsible for human error, typographical mistakes or variation in individual work. This publication is protected under federal copyright laws. Reproduction or distribution of this publication or any other Leisure Arts publication, including publications which are out of print, is prohibited unless specifically authorized. This includes, but is not limited to, any form of reproduction or distribution on or through the internet, including posting, scanning, or e-mail transmission.